MY BROTHER WHO DANCES WITH SUNFLOWERS

Library and Archives Canada Cataloguing in Publication

Title: My brother who dances with sunflowers / Hume Cronyn.
Names: Cronyn, Hume, 1957- author. Description: Poems.

Identifiers: Canadiana (print) 20210103124 | Canadiana (ebook)
20210103167 | ISBN | 9781771611893 (softcover) | ISBN 9781771611909 (EPUB) |
ISBN 9781771611916 (PDF)

Classification: LCC PS8555.R6112 M9 2021 | DDC C811/.54—dc23

Published by Mosaic Press, Oakville, Ontario, Canada, 2023.

MOSAIC PRESS, Publishers
www.mosaic-press.com
Copyright © Hume Cronyn, 2023
Printed and bound in Canada.

Designed by Andrea Tempesta • www.flickr.com/photos/andreatempesta

ONTARIO ARTS COUNCIL
CONSEIL DES ARTS DE L'ONTARIO
an Ontario government agency
un organisme du gouvernement de l'Ontario

Funded by the Government of Canada
Financé par le gouvernement du Canada | Canadä

We acknowledge the Ontario Arts Council
for their support of our publishing program

ONTARIO
CREATES

MOSAIC PRESS
1252 Speers Road, Units 1 & 2, Oakville, Ontario, L6L 5N9
(905) 825-2130 • info@mosaic-press.com • www.mosaic-press.com

MY
BROTHER
WHO
DANCES
WITH
SUNFLOWERS

Hume Cronyn

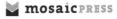 mosaicPRESS

Table of Contents

Preface

Of course, I don't have a brother. Of course, I do have a brother, a brother who is a dreamer, who is anarchic, playful, loves children, goats, has an obsession with elephants, who dances with sunflowers, yammers away to turtles living beneath his bed, who eats peanut butter & bacon sandwiches at midnight with his dinner companion the wind, sings the mysterious songs of giraffes, lives in a house cluttered with ladders. There's a need to have a brother, a sister like this as a source of sustenance, a source of rebellion, a source of survival in a world threatened by wars, environmental catastrophe, technological overwhelm.

It's curious that these poems were written at a great distance from home, while visiting my daughter, Chloe, in Australia. They were written in two outbursts — the first twenty-four when our family travelled across Australia for three weeks, the second twenty-four when my wife & I visited Chloe for two weeks when she was living in Bondi Beach, where I spent a lot of time at the incomparable Gertrude & Alice café. My brother was continually popping up in my mind — an intensity of visitations which I've rarely experienced.

the wind
has an open
invitation
for dinner

Some Facts about My Brother

My brother keeps
a blue fiord from
New Zealand in
his bedroom

Be careful when you walk
around his house
The floors are littered
with spools of thread
& soup spoons with
mysterious bird-
like handles

The earth once had 2 moons
He keeps one of them
in his kitchen
cupboard

There are no drawers
in my brother's house
All his clothes
hang from nails from
the walls like musical
notations

My brother loves the wind
The wind has an open invitation
for dinner
Often they talk long
into the night

My brother wears hats everywhere
& steams around like the vapour
of a teapot
He disappears totally
whenever an argument
breaks out

My brother's door is sunflower yellow
I can be in the darkest mood
but when i walk into his house
a burst of warmth
tickles the soles of my feet
& slowly swims
upwards
Glorious!

My Brother's Singing House

My brother eats porridge
from a singing bowl

The blue tiles in his blue & white-
tiled bathroom
sing

The legs of his old wooden desk
sing

The soles of his shoes
sing

The luminous purple cloud
that lives in the top right-hand
corner of his kitchen
sings

All the windows on the second floor
sing

Most of the lights
sing

The five rivers that
flow through his dreams
sing

His pair of jeans with
the many holes
sing

Sometimes the most exquisite harmonies
usher from his house

Camel Days

My brother loves to sleep

He sleeps at night
He sleeps during the day

You can find him sleeping
at lunchtime
at dinnertime
during the solar eclipse
during the great market meltdown
during the final ticking minutes
                    of the year

He sleeps on the windowsill
He sleeps under his desk
sleeps in the bathtub in his attic
in the canoe in his garden

He eats porridge & cabbage soup
to nourish his dreams

He once slept for seven
solid weeks

When he woke up
he clopped around the house
like a camel
exhausted from his wanderings
through the yellow hills
of the Gobi Desert

it took me days
to convince him
he wasn't a camel

Someone Who Loves Red Licorice
& New Zealand Fiords

My brother rarely leaves his house

He's fanatical that he has
an abundant supply of red licorice
on hand

He loves spaghetti
He is famous for his
spaghetti sculptures

There's stop signs
all over his house
Sometimes he obeys
them

He's been learning to speak
turtle for years
He's not so keen on snapping turtles
His favourite is the spotted lisbon —
especially when it crawls
beneath his bed &
yammers away

The other day
a herd of worms
invaded his living room
He laughed so hard
that the walls were slightly
embarrassed

It's not easy being my brother
No one writes him love letters
The last letter he received
was from the Queen of England
She sent him a recipe
for spinach soup

I hope my brother finds
a soul mate —
someone who loves
red licorice & New Zealand fiords,
who can fathom the mysterious
syntax of turtle,
who understands his
deep cravings to
be a floorboard

Dreams of Building a Tree House

I forgot to tell you this:
my brother's biggest dream
is to build a tree house

It would have 33 windows —
one for each hour of the day

Books would line the walls
& there'd be random stacks
of books towering
like the monolithic slabs
at Stonehenge

Of course one of his spaghetti sculptures
would be a central feature
He would call it the dance
of elephants

My brother loves elephants
but it distresses him that
one has never entered his dreams

His great friend Louis,
the renowned student of corners,
postulates that elephants never enter his dreams
because of my brother's great misfortune
of not being born in Quebec
I tend to agree with him

Brightly-coloured teapots would be perched
in every nook & cranny —
chartreuse, indigo, scarlet, violet &
flaming orange
Teapots remind him of birds

My brother drinks green tea to excess
He intends to paint meticulous spider webs on the walls
to gently cradle the white wings
of his thoughts

Yesterday my brother began to build
his tree house I'll keep you posted

When My Brother Sings

My brother sings the
songs of giraffes

The songs are soft & buzzing
& smell like oranges & mountains

The house literally swoons
when my brother sings
The sun slightly wobbles

Children steal away from school
pitch their shoes into the bushes
& sneak up to my brother's house
so as not to disturb him

But they lose complete control
when they fill up with his singing
& they roll down the hill
in exuberant celebration

for the songs of giraffes
is a long-legged, long-necked affair
which rivals the hallucinations
of love

my
brother
floats
amidst the
cleopatra
rhubarb
leaves

Through a Tiny Rip in His Suitcase

When my brother strolls out of his house
suitcase in his hand

children run after him
Through a tiny rip in his suitcase
days tumble out

sunflower days
hello days
apple days
forgiveness days
hallelujah days

nothing but art days
falling down in the snow
            & laughing days
pyramid days
camel days
change your hat days
remember everything days
somnolent days
shambolic days
get down on your hands & knees days
fried eggs & toast days

Children run after him

(also, a few enlightened adults)

& I, devoted adept & chronicler of his days,
I've been following him for years

He Reminds Me of a Birthday Cake

Some forgotten details I haven't told
you about my brother

Some days he wears nothing but black
His black sombrero is a riot
I've seen him disappear into the night
so beautifully
that I have no trouble in believing
in the birth of water

It's the days when he wears
a pumpkin-coloured glove on his right hand
that I worry about him

His favourite character in literature
is Alyosha in *Brothers Karamazov*

He never wears shoelaces

He says that next year he
will carve a totem pole

I love it when he wears a rubber boot as a hat
He says he looks like a champagne glass
This is one of our major disagreements
I say he looks like a submarine

He reminds me of a birthday cake
lovingly baked by mother
& covered with candles
Each year he burns brighter

He Dances with Sunflowers

My brother loves sunflowers
They stand in gaggles
around his house,
chattering like wise men
discussing the mysteries
of life

The path leading to his house
is lined with the bright faces
of sunflowers welcoming
the occasional visitor

My brother loves their sunny
disposition He calls them
children of the sun
He loves it when they poke
their heads through the open
windows while he rambles on
with the wind

He says sunflowers are concise,
help him to rein in
his wilder circumlocutions

He dances with sunflowers
No one has ever seen him
but like we know that we
have a soul, so we know
that he dances with sunflowers

I have never seen him dance
but once, climbing the hill
to his house, I felt
the earth tremble in delicate
palpitations & I knew that
he was dancing with his
beloved sunflowers

He Floats Amidst the Cleopatra Rhubarb Leaves

How often I have found
my brother sound asleep
in his canoe

This old battered, yellow
canoe with a star-like hole
smashed into its bow
resides in the middle
of his garden

He floats amidst the pale
green cabbage leaves,
amidst the green peppers
& acorn squashes

He floats amidst the drooping
tomatoes, the gentle, flourishing
filigree of asparagus plants,
the knobbly cauliflower heads

He floats past the towering
seven-foot stalk with its clusters
of cone-like buds
(which I thought was
an artichoke plant
till my brother told me
it was a weed)

Why doesn't he dig it up?
He claims it reminds him
of a one-legged stork
& that it sends him hilarious messages
which soften the spikes
of despair that sometimes
grow in him

He floats amidst the Cleopatra
rhubarb leaves, the red-veined
beet leaves, the mouse-like
radish leaves, the frothing bloom
of the flowering purple kale

My brother loves water,
but he says that water is a desert
compared to floating
through his garden

His Sweater Is a Pasture

My brother loves Melville's *Moby Dick*

When he lies down in his canoe
in the middle of his garden
he thinks of Queequeg
who struck by fever
& near death

lay down in his coffin-
canoe to return back
to the starry firmament
of his origins

My brother lies down in his canoe,
particularly when his spirit
is in knots
He watches the clouds

dissolving into one another
flowing like a river
& he feels the knots
in him unwind
& flow

& like Queequeg who rose
up from his coffin
because he remembered
a duty onshore which
he had left undone

so my brother rises up
from his canoe replenished,
his spirit flows like a river,
he rises up laughing
& caterpillars, which have crawled
through the star-shaped hole,

cling greedily to his
green-knitted sweater —
for his sweater is a pasture
for wandering caterpillars

Mice in the Attic

My brother has mice in the attic
but he's convinced that
it's a herd of elephants
tiptoeing across his floor
hungrily searching for the
gateway into his dreams

Usually he dresses
in the most colourful
clothes — the purple of pomegranates,
the orange of pumpkins,
the yellow of lemons —

but there are those days
when he cloaks himself in grey
in praise of elephants

I swear that when I visit him
on those days, his ears
look like elephant ears
He can hear everything
I'm thinking

My brother associates elephants
with clouds Those days
he floats around the house
like an elephant foraging for food
will travel hundreds of miles

His restlessness can be ferocious,
but he doesn't see it that way
He contends he's gathering up thoughts
before he bursts into story

He loves telling the story
how a white elephant appeared
in a dream to the Buddha's mother
the night before she gave birth
to the Buddha

My brother is so obsessed with elephants
that when it snows
he throws open his front door
to welcome the herd
of white elephants
that he swears are just
over the hill

**my
brother
just is is is**

He Just Is Is Is

My brother
my brother my brother
my brother my brother my brother
my brother my brother
my brother

he doesn't manage life
doesn't organize life
life is not to be conquered
subjugated
wrapped up in the mind
& lead to the well

he doesn't lead
nor follow
no aspirations of power
of control
of grandeur

accomplishments mean nothing to him
success
failure
profit
loss
it means nothing to him

to teach/instruct/judge/criticize
no thank you

he just is
is is
is is is
is is
is

is a button
a piece of walnut cake
a parachute
a promise
a bright purple wall
a rambling conversation
a bird's nest
a broom
      that sweeps
      your & my
      stairs

Truth

One day my brother said
that he'd found truth
in the floorboards:

it was a knothole that
resembled the whirlwind
in the dark night
of his mind

Another day he found truth
when the ceiling opened up
& laughed uproariously

Then truth was a burst
of sunshine that played with the dust
under his radiator

Then truth walked through his door —
a blackbird shaking a crust
of bread in his yellow beak

Truth was the sky that fell into his dream
It shattered like pieces of a puzzle
He turned over one piece
It was the face of our mother
at the time of his birth

Truth was his orange pair of clogs

Truth was the memory of his first kiss
that he hung on the wall
like a painting

Truth was his toenails that turned black

Truth was daylight that climbed up his stairs
& tickled his underarms

Truth was the blindness that strikes him once a year
For that day he sits in his canoe
& listens to the hilarious conversations
of his vegetables

My Brother's Swimming Feet

the drums in the river came alive, beaten by the lost ones,
who are not supported by faith — Ingeborg Bachmann

My brother has built a bridge
that crosses the river
snaking behind his house

Often he sits on the bridge
& dips his feet in the water
He hears drums beating &
the soft call of stones

Sometimes, his feet swim
off & explore
the windings of the river

Even at his most sedentary
he always makes a point
of tramping from room to room
in his house

He says he owes it to his feet
& their finely-tuned wanderlust

He doesn't have faith
in the normal sense of the word
but when he hears the drums beating
& the soft call of stones

it is affirmation
that being lost in the world
is no bad thing

for it is the call of the feet,
        irrepressibly beckoned
to the many maps of life

Living in a Piano Note

Those days that my brother
lives in a piano note

Each note is a crystalline globe
He swears he feels like
a baby in the womb

He is born over & over
again

When's he's at his most lyrical
he will talk about
the time he saw a young girl
play Beethoven in the guts
of an abandoned factory

He laughs at our usual pictures
of heaven

Born in a note
wonder grows

like receiving a recipe from the Queen
like a thumbtack found in the paint
like the moon in his cupboard
like the day found in my pen

wonder grows

like the time I found my brother
perched on his roof
imitating the majesty of
his chimney

My Brother's Wandering Pet

My brother's pet lives in his right ankle
In stressful moments he licks
my brother's toes

In euphoric moments he migrates
to his elbow

He's a very gentle animal

When he yelps & yowls
ants crossing the kitchen floor
change direction

the sky achieves an indigo colour
that haunts one to the bone

the one curtain in the house
(my brother hates curtains
but he adores this one
which he says stands like a red rainbow
behind the ramshackle purple couch)
really does look like a red rainbow

the walls look like a field of petunias

My brother's pet rarely sleeps
My brother attributes all his dreams
to the pet's one eye, the other eye
lost on his return journey
from Troy with
Odysseus

My brother's pet —
when he visits my brother's fingers
they glow a pale blue colour
& he's an absolute wizard
on the guitar

Never Sees Himself

My brother never sees himself
when he looks in the mirror

Once he saw a blue button
that had the depth of a deep lake

Another time he saw a chair
with legs as delicate as a summer breeze

a fire that raged in the mouth
of a tiger

a basketful of onions

a red double-decker bus

what about the time he saw
      three beautiful woman
one will become his wife

the time he saw a camel
      white as a ghost

the number seven
as elegant as a pole-vaulter

a spoon that smiled at him

the moon with several bullet holes
through it

the day
the lions
visited my
brother

The Naming of My Brother's Goat

It's inexcusable that I haven't introduced
my brother's pet goat
It follows him around everywhere
& loves Rice Krispies & maple syrup

My brother was working on a farm in Northern Quebec
when he had a premonition that the four-day-old goat
rejected by its mother
was going to be run over by a truck
the next day
So, in order to frustrate fate,
he kidnapped the goat

It's not easy to hitchhike with a goat
He stood outside Quebec City
twelve hours waiting for a ride
He sang every song he knew
& then again

Midnight he got picked up by a truck
hauling celery
Have you ever smelt the combination
of cigarette smoke & slightly rotting celery?
My brother jokes
that it smelt like a Glasgow fog
nestled in a pair
of extremely smelly running shoes

The truck driver asked the name of the goat
My brother not brilliant at those sort of things
said the goat had no name
The truck driver was aghast
said you can't travel around with a goat
with no name

So they riffed all night on possible names
– Edward
– Horatio
– Hampton
– Gulliver
– Jacob
– Jordan
– Joshua
– Bernie
– Sebastian
– Verschoyle
– Verschoyle? Never heard that name
– Name of my Grandfather

Then they had a run on the Cs
– Cassidy
– Constantine
– Caleb
– Cornflake
– Casey
– Carter
– Kidnapped with a C (my brother chuckled over that one)
– Cory
– Cornelius
– Cameron
– Campbell
– Compton
– Clairvoyant

& then they staggered off the Cs onto a random riff of names
– Sinclair
– Lewis
– Morgan
– Tyler
– Jasper
– Heathcliffe
– Albany
– Appleseed
– Appleseed? How can you call a goat Appleseed?
– How can you call an apple seed apple seed?
– True

Then they dipped into the fountain of exotic names
names which had shaped their souls
– Pythagoras
– Socrates
– Mencius
– Lao Tzu
– Homer
– Lucretius
– Patroklos
– Solomon
– Ezekiel
– Ishmael
– Teresias
– Hannibal
– Odysseus

Seven hours of riffing
Finally they flagged & pulled into
a truckers stop for breakfast
When they walked in an old-style jukebox
was quietly playing Love Me Tender
The truck driver ecstatically exclaimed, That's the perfect name

– What?
– Love Me Tender
– Not bad my brother said, but not quite
– Elvis
– No
– Presley
– No
– Then he stuttered for the first time all night, J... J... J...
– No, I'm not going to call my goat Jupiter
– J... J... J... JUKEBOX!
– Jukebox... brilliant!

& Jukebox prancing beside these two
intrepid name givers
jumped straight up in the air
& did a jukebox dance
that only a goat named Jukebox
could ever do

Pink Lightning

My brother has constructed a pond
beside this unusual outcropping of rock
marked by a pink zigzag
running through it

He calls it his pink lightning rock
He will often read here
overlooking the pond
with its new family of mallards

My brother watches them for hours,
says they're tracking the movement
of his soul

Ants will scurry up his legs
but he never seems to mind
their ticklish migration
across his body

Butterflies land on his shoulders
Once in the evening this
most beautiful white moth
with its orange & silver ribbed body
landed on the back of his
outstretched hand

Sometimes chipmunks run across
his feet

What about the time a deer
nibbled at his ear
He was absolutely ecstatic
& for weeks talked about
the tenderness of that nuzzle

But what I noticed was
that from that moment
there was a perceptible broadening
of his gentleness

The Day the Lions Visited My Brother

After school children will run
over to my brother's place
to see what he's reading

They always wear a piece
of clothing that is white
because my brother never sees
white as plain white
In his mind it is always
delphinium white

Delphinium is one of his favourite words

The children wait for him to say
What a wonderful delphinium white
hat you are wearing,
or, that raincoat reminds me of the
delphinium white eggs
of the spotted lisbon

It's a ritual: for the children love hearing
him say the word delphinium
It has all the mystery of
the Delphic oracles

Then they ask him to read
a passage from what he's reading
He declaims from a poem
by Christopher Smart

The LION roars HIMSELF complete
from head to tail

Oh what a glorious hubbub greets my brother
The children begin to roar
turbulent rumblings of soul truth
they get down on their hands & knees
they surround my brother & roar
COMPLETE from head to tail

Hello Poem

My brother once lived
in a squat in England

He has told me many stories
about it. Climbing Everest
pales in comparison

Today he wants me to say
hello to his friends

hello Mick

hello Katrin

hello Patricia

hello Eddie

hello Chris
who from his third-story window
lowered notes on a fishing line
to the unappreciated
front door

hello Brian
who mounted bicycle frames
on his wall
& slept bicycle dreams

hello Graham
who looked after the elephants
in the London Zoo,
who always smelt of elephants
& spoke with floppy-eared
zaniness

My Brother Laughs Roundly at My Habits

My brother has a brother
(that's me!!!)
who puts everything into
books

For decades I have madly clipped
newspaper articles, pasted
them on blue paper
& gathered them in innumerable
red binders

For decades I have typed up
favourite poems & made them
into books

I have books of my favourite quotes,
books of journals, photographs,
books of recorded dreams,
books of my first drafts,
books of final drafts

books! books! everything put
in books My brother laughs
roundly at my habits

His life & dreams live outside of books
They are wild & woolly creatures
& he hasn't the slightest need
to enclose them between
covers

He throws open his windows
for he does not want to contain
his singing
And when the wind comes for dinner:
in the middle of the night
they whip up a stack
of peanut butter & bacon
sandwiches

No need for books,
his sumptuous spirit
lives outside the covers,
feasting on the bright air
& the whispering cornfields
of night

My Brother Makes a Toast

My brother calls together his friends
They sit around a table draped
with a red table cloth
Red candles burn
throwing red shadows against
the walls My brother
makes a toast

My friends, we are beautifully crazy
We carry the moon under our arms
There is always at least one acorn
in our pockets

In our most lonely moments
we dance with sunflowers
Our skin is white as birch
Our words swim like exotic fish
shocking the barren moments

My deep companions,
we don't often drink
but when we drink
we drink to the heart of life
In rare moments we touch the beating
Sometimes we sing with it

My dear companions,
when I wear my boot hat
I am both a submarine
& a champagne glass
I believe in the deep truths
but our discoveries mean nothing
unless they are shared

Rimbaud believed in the derangement
of the senses
We drink for other reasons
We have worlds to share,
to dispute, moments of flight

And when we discuss dreams
the air takes on the shimmer
of pollen, our ideas
are as light as butterflies,
& our laughter? Our laughter
delights the birds

my
brother's
breathing
bones

My Brother the Whale

My brother loves swimming
in the rain. While everyone
ducks inside or takes cover
beneath umbrellas,

he's flopping about
in the middle of his pond —
plip-plop the dance
of raindrops
bouncing all around him,
bouncing off his bald
head

He calls rain
threads to
the Mysterious Source;
swimming in his pond,
baptism in the holy
fount

When I arrive
sheltered beneath my tattered
umbrella

he's thrashing about
like a whale
Rolling onto his back,
he shoots up lofty spumes
of water

then bursts into strains
of hallelujah,
glorious, lilting, drawn-out
ululations of hallelujah

He says every whale knows
Jeff Buckley's Hallelujah
Hallelujah, hallelujah, hallelujah, hallelujah

My brother, my brother the whale

My Brother's Breathing Bones

My brother loves staring out
at calm water —
sheet of unrippled water,
mirrored smoothness,
it calms his mind

He loves the sense that underneath
something is breathing — intake of breath,
outtake of breath —
the breathing of an inner spirit

particularly at twilight
when the world begins to throw off
the shackles of busyness,
slow descent into stillness

Sometimes, when
the setting sun burns
its luminous path across
the slate grey, turquoise-tinged
water of his pond

he sees himself walk that path
(from where he is sitting)
to the middle of the pond

He also sees another from the
opposite shore do the same

& as he watches he realizes
the other is himself!
& the other merges when they meet
in the middle

There are times he has seen four or five
of himselves come from different angles,
merge in the middle

In those moments,
even his bones breathe with
the water

Inside Out

Ha! When my brother
wears his clothes
inside out
he's the warmest person
in the world

He's a small sun

I follow him around
the house basking
in his warmth

His jeans he's patched
from the inside
I love the polka-dot
patches —
purple & white
amber & vermilion

Needless to say, he's worn
his t-shirts for years
They're mouse-bitten
around the collar,
rips under the armpits

but when he wears them
inside out,
they look like entirely
different creatures

Usually he's barefooted,
but if he wears socks
they're never the same colour
inside out
the colourful tangle
of lose threads

Inside out
He says it's like
opening a drawer
& dumping the contents
on the floor

The joy of revelation

Ladders

It's a riot how many
ladders my brother
has lying around
the house,

wooden ladders,

he moves them around
so often
that I think
they're wandering
animals

Except for one
(each rung painted
a different colour)
rising up
to a perch
that resembles a
bird's nest

My brother reads here
looking down
into the living room
with its purple couch,
fireplace,
pell-mell scatter of logs
around the hearth

the wind billowing
the one curtain

He reads,
takes wing

Goodbye ladders!

& if I come by,
I don't disturb him
I leave him a note
(he loves notes)

I jot down a few lines
of what I'm reading
It's amazing how often
our readings intersect

Raindrops

The children love tumbling
about my brother's
ramshackle house

They have a sixth
sense when he needs
his country of aloneness,
but when his front door
is flapping in the wind
it's an open invitation

The children clamber
over the couches,
climb up ladders
They love the nest,
chirp like a brood of
young birds

They rearrange the ladders,
lay them across from couch
to armchair — bridges
to cross death-defying
gorges

They load up Jukebox
with packs,
hike up my brother's
Himalayan staircase,
yammering away in
imagined Nepalese

Other times they climb
the ladder to the attic
Tents are pitched
Jukebox is the last camel
standing as they stagger
across the Sahara,
fearless Bedouins in search
of a life-saving well

Ha! When my brother sees
them dropping down a rope,
sliding past the kitchen window,
pretending they're raindrops
watering the thirsty cauliflowers,
he hoots with laughter

My Brother's Flying House

How dangerous it is when my brother
overhears a snippet of conversation

"You know my house flies?"
"How do you get it to stop?"

Soon his house is awash with drawings —
tables, floors, couches,
even one found in the refrigerator

Oh, what a project!
All the children caught up
in the wildness
They construct a pair of wings
with a pattern of colourful
wooden shingles

They attach them to the house,
& with an ingenuous arrangement of pulleys
they can be lowered
flush against the wall

But when they are raised,
what journeys they take

They cross the boiling green
canopy of the Congo Basin

the savage dust storms
of the Kalahari Desert

the white-capped North Atlantic
studded with Icelandic fishing fleets

the golden tasseled cornfields
of the boundless American Midwest

the lonely brokered call of seagulls
wheeling off the shores of Patagonia

"How do you get it to stop?"
That's not so easy to answer

the
whispered
elephants
of song

Green Mountain Poem

Today my brother saw
a green mountain
strolling across
his pond

Beautiful!

as only a green
mountain
can be

End of story!
he wouldn't elaborate

I tried to understand it
in my own way
Was it a hallucination?
Phantasmagoria?

Was it from indigestion?
A bilious liver?
A trick of light?
A longing for mystery?

What had he been reading?
Was he dreaming?
Trying to shock me into
a new way of seeing?

I will probably never understand,
but I believe my brother

& am comforted by the fact
that he saw a green
mountain

strolling

across the water
September 13th, 2018

my brother's birthday

Listening to the Wind

My brother listens to the wind
as it blows across his pond
where the green mountain
strolls

It blows
The leaves swish & swash
in their jubilant
dance

He feels encapsulated in the wind
Where does it come from?

The same place as he comes from
Mother womb
It is the whisper of
children

My brother basks in the wind
It tickles his cheeks
It tumbles his lips
It fizzes his hair

It brightens his eyes
It is beginnings

It's the scent of peaches
the sputtered sand of deserts
the fractured appointments with destiny
the whispered elephants of song

The wind begins my brother
See him cartwheeling across
the lawn
Ho! Like a green mountain
strolling on water

Backwards

There are days when my brother
wakes up & decides
he'll spend the day walking
backwards

Backwards to the washroom
to brush his teeth,
backwards down the stairs
carefully! carefully!

He studies the dust in the
junctures of the stairs,
watches the journey
of a ladybug

Backwards into the kitchen,
backwards to the frying pan
hanging from the wall
like the chime of a grandfather
clock

Before he cracks his eggs
on the lip of the frying pan,
backwards into time
(cooking eggs with Dad)

Backwards out his back door,
backwards he stands in the sun,
the back of his neck warmed

He notices the back of his house,
all the windows opened
to different heights —
asymmetrical invitations to
the wind

Sudden thoughts of beginning
his day with dinner
Breakfast at midnight!

two fried eggs two glorious suns:
preamble to the entrance
into night

My Brother's Sneeze

My brother's sneeze is
a shattered window

is a downfall of spoons
crashing on the floor

is a herd of buffalo trampling
through a bed of thistles

is a panic attack
midst the champagne glasses

is a pharmacy bursting
with laughter

is a hurricane of light bulbs
hurtling against a wall

is a pink scarf dragged
from a carton of milk

is a choir of caterpillars
waking up the leaves

is a parade of bees
nibbling at the moon

is a clatter of knitting needles
tumbling in a dryer

is a squadron of airplanes crashing
into a forest of chandeliers

my brother's sneeze —
it blows out his windows

it storms the quietude of his bedroom
it floods his basement

a howl of wet laughter

A Fleeting Nostalgia

My brother wakes up
to the song of birds

First, a two note
clarion call
cuts the morning
like an alarm
clock

(which my brother
has disposed of
years ago)

If he was to give
a shape to these calls
it would be two
bullet holes
bursting the moon
of his dreams

Then, there's a
explosion of chirping
as if a mother bird is
feeding her young

Then, a stabbing squawk

Then, a hullabaloo
of squeaking

Then, a cacophony
of cackling
like an inundation
of fishhooks under
his pillow

My brother begins
to fondly remember
his alarm clock

My Brother Explores the Dark

My brother believes there are many
layers of dark

The deepest layer that he's traveled to —
slate black with shades of livid purple
Several times he has been there

The odd sensation of skimming
as if in a sailboat
with a coal-black sail,
running with the wind

& each time there were thoughts
of his last minutes with our dying mother;
the startling sense

that he's become the materialization
of her dream self —
the mystery of it & the
responsibility

He knows there's deeper levels
but he feels unprepared
Perhaps later, but always
the fear there's a darkness
from which he will never
return

he respects darkness
like he respects water

Lightness is also a truth
Maybe a greater truth

He is always mindful of this

one-fifth
of his dreams
are inhabited
by ants

Jukebox's Desolation

My brother
is sitting outside
the sun beating down
the sky sapphire
blue

He soaks up
the sun
grows warm
in the chilly
breeze

grows warmer

& warmer

till he becomes
sunbeam
translucent
sunbeam

Jukebox
runs frantically around
him
for my brother has become
translucent
sunbeam

invisible message from
the sun

indivisible
oneness

& Jukebox
is utterly desolate
Where has my brother
gone?

Oh, just a momentary
transport
A moment of
being

sunbeam

Nose Poem

My brother has one mirror
in his house

The other morning I came flying
through the door
He was standing in front of the mirror
laughing

Laughing, he kept repeating
"Welcome home my nose"

I'm rarely surprised by my brother
(I have years of experience)
but I was a bit astonished

What's up? I said

Last night I had a dream, he said
I was sleeping in a cave,
one of the walls
was a wall of noses

A wall of noses?

Yes, there was a fleshy nose
an aquiline nose
a hooked nose
a snub nose
even a runny one

In my dream I laughed —
noses are such odd creatures,
especially, when detached from the face

Then I saw my nose
on the wall My nose!

I woke up, patted my face
My nose was still there,
but I still couldn't believe it

so I ran to the mirror
I find it hilarious that I
couldn't trust my touch

Ants

My brother knows that I'm
writing poems about him,
& being a deeply subversive
person

he wants to subvert the project

He throws a word at me
like a ball
Begin your poem with
the word *ants*

Ants, his hair is the colour
of ants

His one bruised toenail
is the colour of ants

Ants walk through his dreams
His rough estimation
is that one-fifth of his dreams
are inhabited by
ants

but never elephants!

A troop of ants is stationed
in his kitchen
They feast on the cake crumbs
which litter the floor

There's the ants which change
direction when he sings,
the ants which tickle his toes
when he's nodding off in
the living room

There's the ants of forgetting
the ants of divination
the ants of anarchic punctuation
the ants of blinding sunsets

They're a real part of my brother's life
these small industrious creatures —
handmaidens to the coming of the
elephants

Tiptoeing

Oh! Oh! it's one of those days
My brother is tiptoeing
around the house

He says the couch
needs quiet

The windows need
quiet

The one mirror
the stairs
the pots & pans need
quiet

His jeans hanging from
a nail need
quiet

His hat jauntily
perched on the
coat rack needs
quiet

The crack in the wall
the partially-closed door
the turtle under his bed
need quiet

the stand-up lamp
the Persian rugs
the pens on his desk
they all need
quiet

for they need to
dream a dream
of repose

& my brother lies down
in the middle of
the floor
& bathes
in the uncanny
silence

My Brother Reflects on Old Age

My brother watches an old man
walk past

The old man hobbles forth
into the narrowing light

His eyes are as dead
as burnt-out comets,
his face wrinkled up
like a walnut

His ill-fitting trousers
drag on the sidewalk,
his white jacket stained
by a teardrop of spilt
coffee

One hand grips
a pale blue plastic bag
with a pound of melting
butter

& half a dozen eggs,
one bleeding through a crack
a viscous yellow yolk

In his other hand he holds
a crumpled Kleenex
as if it were a cane

His wild & rumpled hair
excavated by the wind

He's mumbling, *He restoreth
my soul; he leadeth me*

All his life my brother
has had a particular attraction
to the young & the old —
he considers them
bookends
illuminating the mysterious journey
of life

Ambling Down the Road

One of my
brother's closest friends,
a 103-year-old
Buddhist monk,
talks about
gradually ambling
down the road towards
the wheel of
reincarnation

My brother loves
the sense of
ambling —

not limping,
stumping a cane,
or dragging his
lumpen body

rather the lightness,
fearlessness,
of ambling

My brother pays
special attention
to his friend's
meditations
on the need
to contain displeasure,
anger &
complaining

My brother does not
believe in
overriding devotion
but is thankful
for the deep currents
of wisdom

running
through all
religions

my
brother's
ocean
pilgrimages

Canoe Dream

My brother had a dream
that he was sleeping
in his canoe
in the wild-tossed sea
of his garden

The bottom of the
canoe
was covered
with grass

luxuriant sprouting
of grass,
tender shoots
of an ineffable
colour of green
tending towards
apple-green

The shoots of grass
were holding him
up,
holding him in
their arms

in the gentlest
sleep
one could ever
imagine

A sleep of love

& when he woke
up he broke
into tears
for he had never
experienced
such overwhelming
love

My Brother's Ocean Pilgrimages

I've talked about my brother's
pilgrimages to the
ocean

He's just returned from
one,
the turquoise water
that reflects the plenitude
of soul-life

the gathering of water
as it bulks up
& crashes
into a girdle
of
frothing white

slides
towards the amber-
coloured sand

My brother follows the beach
around
to the headland,
jut
of ferocious rock,

as the waves
crash,
throw up a fantastic
spray

of white flowers

slide of ocean
slide of turquoise
slide of froth

much like soul-life
that blanches
the firmament
of bones

Pulling Down Walls

Walls block the wind,
block the sunshine,
birds, even
the turtles

The roof is no better

Doors are a small
improvement
They swing open
& shut

Too often they are
closed

Windows are holes
in the wall
My brother often leaves
them open
The wind visits
Birds fly in

for they have a
special affinity
for my brother's
ladders & one
high-backed yellow
armchair
inherited from
our mother

& when sunshine floods in
& lights up the house

my brother claims
it is like the self
when it pulls down
its walls
& welcomes in
the world

The Laughing Buddha Poem

Again the weather forecasters
have called for rain
& thunder showers

Instead it's a beautiful
sunny day
the sky cobalt blue
only a few clouds

On the horizon
wispy ball-like clouds,
except one bulky one
that looks like a
rhinoceros

My brother's sitting outside
the trees lightly swaying
leaves rustling

My brother drifting
in his mind
decides to add himself
to the cloudscape

So there he is moving
across the sky,
sitting cross-legged like
the Laughing Buddha
(though my brother is in continual
argument with Buddhism
he loves the meditative
pose)

He is floating across the sky:
the rhinoceros
the Laughing Buddha
& some wispy clouds
looking like donuts

floating (on a day
that the forecasters predicted
rain)
as happy as a
cloud
in a blue
sky

Rustling Rhubarb Leaves

My brother opens
the bedroom window

Tonight the wind,
his friend, his accomplice
in all-night word
marathons,
withholds his
visitation

My brother listens
to the gentle lapping
of his pond,
the slap of water
against the rock

He listens to the hum
of the stars

the train as
it throws off its haunting
hoot

the cabbages whispering
to each other

the rhubarb leaves
rustling in the breeze
like elephant ears

I'm going to forego a joke
about my brother's obsession
with elephants
but it's a fact
he's planted rhubarb
because its leaves resemble
elephant ears

& when the rhubarb leaves
rustle
my brother trembles
in his bed

My Brother's Dream
Announcing the Coming of the Elephants

He was trudging across the desert,
almost doubled over, carrying
the large blue ball of the
ocean on his back

He walked for 3 days & 3 nights,
came to a grove of palm trees
huddled in the glaring moonlight
In the heart of the grove,
a herd of white antelope
were calmly sleeping

A pale blue stream
threaded its way past the
antelope My brother
uttered some words to
the antelope They responded
with a soft humming sound —

permission for him to follow
the stream In no time
he emerged from the grove
The heat was unbearable
He felt he'd walked into
a raging fire

He wanted to put down the ocean,
fall into a deep sleep
The stream was a mere trickle

He was picking his way through
a wild stretch of stones, striated,
grey-coloured stones
He fell to his knees

With great effort he got up again
The stones started to sing harmonies
like he'd never heard before

Music surged through his body,
the ocean on his back as light
as a feather